Letters from the Road

Photographs by Gabrielle Keller

Text by Ethan Berry

Foreword by **Anthony Rotundo**

This book is a journal of thoughts and pictures, by Ethan Berry and Gabrielle Keller, who both came back to motorcycles after a long absence. Their dialogue started at Freeman Cycles in Beverly, MA which became an ideal setting for extended conversations that went beyond motorcycles and the traditional imagery associated with them. They continued to communicate while traveling, one writing from the road, and the other photographing in a motorcycle repair shop. The interplay between the male voice (the written work) and the female voice (the pictures) created an intensely personal narrative that eventually became a conversation in itself. The conversation moves forward as a series of moments in time, brief encounters of feeling, thought, and image that resonate across pages and miles.

Special thanks for their support on this project:

John Bick, the staff at Freeman Cycles & the Team Freeman group of riders, Beverly, MA
Lillian Lambrechts, Art Curator, FleetBoston Financial, Boston, MA
Cornelia Fellowship Grant, Montserrat College of Art, Beverly, MA
Elisabeth Schumacher, Köln, Germany

Letters From the Road ©*2004 Gabrielle Keller*
photographs ©*2004 Gabrielle Keller*
text ©*2004 Ethan Berry*
foreword ©*2004 Anthony Rotundo*

ISBN *0-9755337-0-3*

book design by Gabrielle Keller
printed by Kirkwood Printing, Wilmington, MA, USA

All rights reserved. No part of this book may be reproduced or transmitted in any form or by any means electronic or mechanical, including photocopying, recording or by any information storage or retrieval system, without permission in writing from the copyright owner.

For information regarding distribution, marketing and bulk purchases,
or to order additional copies of this book, contact: gabriellekellerbooks.com

Anthony Bourdain

If Americans deserve a place in history as a creative people, it is not because we treasure the arts or cherish utopian thought. Rather, the creativity of our American nation has come from its inventors. We Americans have so prized the materialism, the process, that we have poured our imaginative energies through our machine shops and laboratories in quantities that are uniquely American. A prosaic nation admires the earth-bound dream. We love practical solutions to material problems that seem to elude our dreams, or are our machines.

The machines become vehicles for our dreams of freedom. The light bulb takes us from the darkness, the telephone and television takes us from isolation, airplane, the computer cuts us loose from the limitations of our own memories. But the most American of dreams is the one that moves us at will from place to place. The Mayflower, the covered wagon, Huck's raft—all these are part of our national mythology. But we have staked our deepest aspirations on the powerful machine. Inventive is the swiftness of dreams: the train, the car, the airplane, the rocket, and the most personal of these, the motorcycle.

The images and text in the following pages give us the motorcycle and the shop that nurtures it, the dream machine and its cradle. If the shop is the home of dreams and the motorcycle is their vehicle, the dreams involved are not uniformly American. They rhapsodize masculinity. The machine shop is a male-centered space, much like the salon or the barber shop, and the only place for a woman in the mythology of the motorcycle is on the back, with her arms around the man in front of her, the subordinate partner in the pursuit of his dreams. And yet, while the shop and the motorcycle may be about men's dreams, the romance requires the work of a woman as much as a man.

In 1955, Walker Evans published a photo-essay on tools in *Fortune* Magazine. Photographed against dark backgrounds, the wire cutters, wrenches and pliers shone with metallic clarity. Their outlines were perfect, their surfaces untarnished by the scars that tools with a history would wear to signal the user or the use. His photographs gave shape to the machine shop dream as an end in itself. Glowing as if from internal sources of light, these tools were not just visual representations of themselves—they are images of the Platonic ideal of the tool.

Gabrielle Keller's photographs of tools are all context. Marked and scored, these tools are made of their own use. We see too the hands that use them, the shapes that are fit for them. Most important, we see the motorcycle that they fix: motorcycles in motion, motorcycles at rest, motorcycles in storage. We see the component parts of the motorcycle, the pieces of the dream. But we see them, together with the metal shavings and the oil spots that are by-products of the machine's overall condition.

While Gabrielle was in the shop with her cameras, and Barry was riding his motorcycle from Massachusetts to Pennsylvania, as he traveled, he wrote his reflections back to Gabrielle, sometimes in relation to the photographs she sent him, mostly in relation to the experience of his trip. In his reflections, he took apart his thoughts and spread them out for inspection, as if he were back in the shop taking apart his BMW. The exercise of the machine process consciousness, trying to understand the workings of the mechanism.

This book is a journal of thoughts and pictures, by Ethan Berry and Gabrielle Keller, who both came back to motorcycles after a long absence. Their dialogue started at Freeman Cycles in Beverly, MA, which became an ideal setting for extended conversations that went beyond motorcycles and the traditional imagery associated with them. They continued to communicate while traveling, one writing from the road, and the other photographing in a motorcycle repair shop. The interplay between the male voice (the written story) and the female voice (the pictures) created an intensely personal narrative that eventually became a conversation in itself. The conversation moves forward as a series of moments in time, brief encounters of feeling, thought, and image that resonate across pages and miles.

Special thanks for their support on this project:

*Bob Miller, Beverly American Cycle, the Team Freeman group of riders, Beverly, MA
Edwin Tamibrelli, The Garage Motorcycle Restoration, Salem, MA
Cornelia Fellowship Grant, Montserrat College of Art, Beverly, MA
Elisabeth Schumacher, Köln, Germany*

Letters from the Road ©2004 Gabrielle Keller
photographs ©2004 Gabrielle Keller
text ©2004 Ethan Berry
foreword ©2004 Matthew Rotundo

ISBN 0-9753728-1-3

book design by Gabrielle Keller
printed by Kirkwood Printers, Wilmington, MA USA

All rights reserved. No part of this book may be used or transmitted in any form or by any means, electronic or mechanical, including photocopying, recording, or by any information storage and retrieval system, without permission in writing from the copyright owner.

For information regarding distribution, image reproduction, purchasing, or to order additional copies of this book, please inquire at the book's home.

Foreword by **Anthony Rotundo**

If Americans deserve a place in history as a creative people, it is not because we treasure the arts or cherish utopian thought. Rather, the creativity of our pragmatic nation has come from its inventors. We Americans have so prized the material and the practical that we have poured our imaginative energies through our machine shops and laboratories in quantities that are uniquely American. A prosaic nation admires the earth-bound dream. We love practical solutions to material problems that seem insoluble. Our dreams are in our machines.

The machines become vehicles for our dreams of freedom. The light bulb frees us from the darkness, the telephone and television liberate us from limitations of place, the computer cuts us loose from the limitations of our own memories. But the most American of dreams is the one that moves us at will from place to place. The Mayflower, the covered wagon, Huck's raft - all these are part of our national mythology. But we have saved our deepest fascination for the powerful machines that give us the swiftness of dreams - the train, the car, the airplane, the rocket, and the most personal of these, the motorcycle.

The images and text in the following pages give us the motorcycle and the shop that nurtures it...the dream machine and its cradle. If the shop is the home of dreams and the motorcycle is their vehicle, the dreams involved are not just distinctly American. They are distinctly male. The machine shop is a man's space just as much as the saloon or the barber shop, and the only place for a woman in the mythology of the motorcycle is on the back, with her arms around the man in front of her...the subordinate partner in the pursuit of his dreams. And yet, while the shop and the motorcycle may be about men's dreams, the image and the text here are the work of a woman as much as a man.

In 1955, Walker Evans published a photo essay on tools in Fortune Magazine. Photographed against plain dark backgrounds, the wire cutters, wrenches, and pliers shone with metallic clarity. Their outlines were perfect, their surfaces unmarked by use. They were tools without context, tools with no sign of the user or the use. The photographs gave shape to the machine shop dream as an end in itself. Glowing as if from internal sources of light, these tools were not just visual representations of themselves - they were images of the Platonic ideal of the tool.

Gabrielle Keller's photographs of tools are all context. Marked and scored, these tools are maps of their own use. We see, too, the hands that use them, that fix them, that care for them. Most importantly, we see the motorcycles that they fix...motorcycles in motion, motorcycles at rest, motorcycles in storage. We see the component parts of the motorcycle, the pieces of the dream…and we see them together with the metal shavings and the oil stains that are the by-products of the machine's overall condition.

While Gabrielle was in the shop with her camera, Ethan Berry was riding his motorcycle from Massachusetts to Pennsylvania. As he traveled, he wrote his reflections back to Gabrielle - sometimes in reaction to the photographs she sent him, mostly in relation to the experience of his trip. In his reflections, he took apart his thoughts and spread them out for inspection, as if he were back in the shop taking apart his BMW. He examined the marks and grooves of consciousness, trying to understand the workings of the mechanism.

The text and images here seem to place man and woman in a familiar relation to each other. Gabrielle is "back home" at the place where motorcycles are nurtured, where they go to rest. Ethan is "out in the world," riding from place to place, living the dream of mobility. In the classic version of our national myth, the man seeks the freedom of movement as a way to escape the confines of domesticity - and the women who preside over it. Gabrielle and Ethan are playing out the fundamental gender drama of the last two centuries in America.

Or so it seems. Gender dramas never lack complexity, and the one played out in the pages that follow contradicts itself in countless ways. The shop may be the place that nurtures the motorcycle and renews its health, but it is still, after all, a male space. A woman riding her own motorcycle is a more common sight than a woman hanging out in a motorcycle shop. When Gabrielle looks through her camera into odd corners of the shop, she is working from an alternative gender script, exploring the male mysteries of the dream in the machine.

Likewise, Ethan is varying the classic gender role as much as he is playing it. He wrote home constantly, in clear violation of the rules for the American male quest. Huck never sent Aunt Polly a letter - Ahab didn't write home. (Though reality often contradicted myth. Thoreau's mother visited the cabin at Walden Pond, and he went home for Sunday dinner.) And Ethan didn't just write to Gabrielle - he opened his thoughts and feelings to her. In fact, when Gabrielle examines the dark corners of the shop and Ethan ventures into the dark corners of his mind, the two come back to each other with reports - whether in words or images - of what they've found in the shadows. They are building a connection, a kind of relationship, each offering bits of perception to the other.

This is not the classic story of the machine shop or the motorcycle. The dream of freedom, the creative stroke that solves a material problem - these have never been the stuff of intimacy. To be sure, the maintenance of a close relationship involves the friction of hard edges, the striations and pock marks of long use. But it is mercy, not motor oil, that smooths the abrasions of intimacy. What is it, asks Ethan, "that allows one part of an engine to mesh or glide past another, thousands, millions of times? What are the relationships that make this behavior predictable?" The certainty that Ethan seeks may be possible in the shop, but intimacy allows no precision tooling.

We know the mythologies of the motorcycle and the machine shop - those dreams are male ones. There are also mythologies of intimate relationships. They are the stuff of romance novels and Hollywood endings - we consider them female dreams. They are unlike our male dreams in that they emphasize intimacy, embrace, domesticity. And yet both dreams, the male and the female, express our yearning for a boundlessness that we can never have - the dream of a freedom without limits, the dream of a romance that lasts "happily ever after."

But the dreams are just that. They are never fully realized - and neither are our ideals of gender. We may imagine "male" and "female" as principles with perfect separation. But, as lived, those principles always leak their contents into one another. There is no truly "male" man, no completely "female" woman, no way to keep the girls from playing boys' games or vice versa. Gabrielle and Ethan may seem to be working from an alternative gender script, but, in truth, we all do. Like Walker Evans's perfect tools, the ideal gender script may exist in some Platonic form, but, in the end neither the tool nor the script provides an answer. Each must serve a user and the user's special use. We mark up our gender scripts to suit our needs.

Anthony Rotundo is the author of American Manhood: Transformations in Masculinity from the Revolution to the Modern Era *(Basic Books, 1993). He is a teacher of history at Phillips Academy in Andover, Massachusetts, where he is Co-Director of the Brace Center for the Study of Gender.*

The text and images here seem to place man and woman in a familiar relation to each other. Gabrielle is "back home" at the place where motorcycles are nurtured, where they go to rest. Ethan is "out in the world," riding from place to place, living the dream of mobility. In the classic version of our national myth, the man seeks the freedom of movement as a way to escape the confines of domesticity - and the women who preside over it. Gabrielle and Ethan are playing out the fundamental gender drama of the last two centuries in America.

Or so it seems. Gender dramas never lack complexity, and the one played out in the pages that follow contradicts itself in countless ways. The shop may be the place that nurtures the motorcycle and renews its health, but it is still, after all, a male space. A woman riding her own motorcycle is a more common sight than a woman hanging out in a motorcycle shop. When Gabrielle looks through her camera into odd corners of the shop, she is working from an alternative gender script, exploring the male mysteries of the dream in the machine.

Likewise, Ethan is varying the classic gender role as much as he is playing it. He wrote home constantly, in clear violation of the rules for the American male quest. Huck never sent Aunt Polly a letter - Ahab didn't write home. (Though reality often contradicted myth. Thoreau's mother visited the cabin at Walden Pond, and he went home for Sunday dinner.) And Ethan didn't just write to Gabrielle - he opened his thoughts and feelings to her. In fact, when Gabrielle examines the dark corners of the shop and Ethan ventures into the dark corners of his mind, the two come back to each other with reports - whether in words or images - of what they've found in the shadows. They are building a connection, a kind of relationship, each offering bits of perception to the other.

This is not the classic story of the machine shop or the motorcycle. The dream of freedom, the creative stroke that solves a material problem - these have never been the stuff of intimacy. To be sure, the maintenance of a close relationship involves the friction of hard edges, the striations and pock marks of long use. But it is mercy, not motor oil, that smooths the abrasions of intimacy. What is it, asks Ethan, "that allows one part of an engine to mesh or glide past another, thousands, millions of times? What are the relationships that make this behavior predictable?" The certainty that Ethan seeks may be possible in the shop, but intimacy allows no precision tooling.

We know the mythologies of the motorcycle and the machine shop - those dreams are male ones. There are also mythologies of intimate relationships. They are the stuff of romance novels and Hollywood endings - we consider them female dreams. They are unlike our male dreams in that they emphasize intimacy, embrace domesticity. And yet both dreams, the male and the female, express our yearning for a boundlessness that we can never have - the dream of a freedom without limits, the dream of a romance that lasts "happily ever after."

But the dreams are just that. They are never fully realized - and neither are our ideals of gender. We may imagine "male" and "female" as principles with perfect separation. But, as lived, those principles always leak their contents into one another. There is no truly "male" man, no completely "female" woman, no way to keep the girls from playing boys' games or vice versa. Gabrielle and Ethan may seem to be working from an alternative gender script, but, in truth, we all do. Like Walker Evans's perfect tools, the ideal gender script may exist in some Platonic form, but, in the end neither the tool nor the script provides an answer. Each must serve a user and the user's special use. We mark up our gender scripts to suit our needs.

Anthony Rotundo is the author of American Manhood: Transformations in Masculinity from the Revolution to the Modern Era *(Basic Books, 1993). He is a teacher of history at Phillips Academy in Andover, Massachusetts, where he is Co-Director of the Brace Center for the Study of Gender.*

Am I ever prepared for the times when meaning grabs me and shakes me loose? She says these bikes are abandoned. I say they look mysteriously timeless. She says they represent power and speed in repose. I say they look like they emerge from the dark corner of the shed. I am familiar with this place, this state of things collected and put aside, of abundance and sadness at the same time.

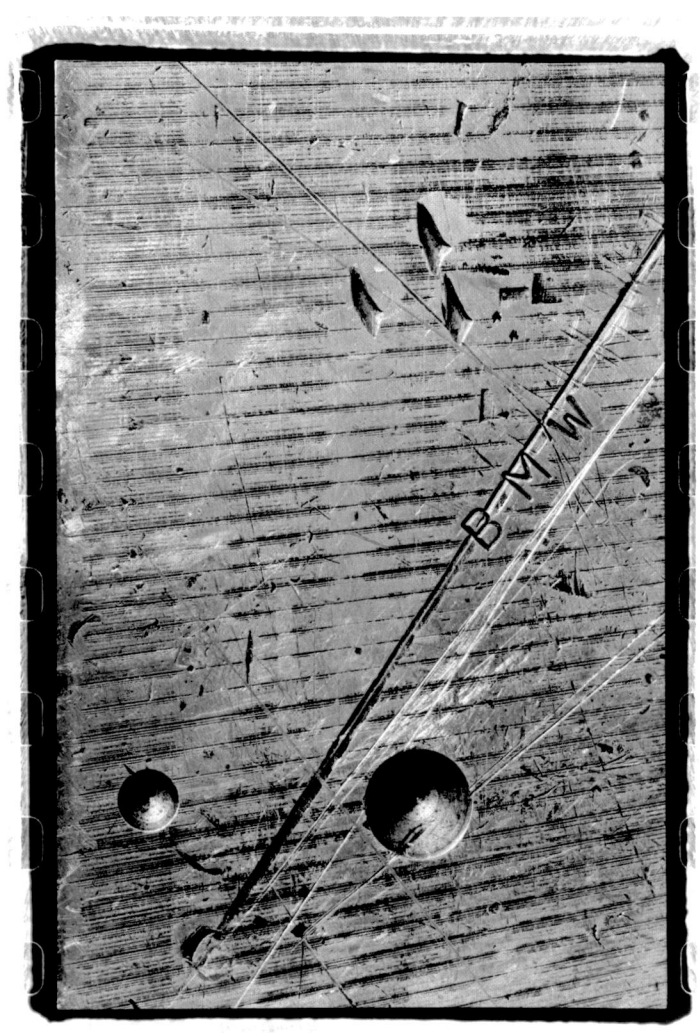

Riding is like dreaming, projecting yourself forward, focusing outward. Sometimes there are so many distractions that the dream is hard to sustain. Moving around the track black streaks go off at distracting angles where bikes and cars have gone out of control. These marks don't register until later when I'm standing in the pits. I see the skidmarks and bruises and ambulance crew lounging nearby and I realize how serious this activity is.

Driving is like dreaming, projecting yourself forward, focusing outward. Sometimes there are so many distractions that the dream is hard to sustain. Moving around the track black streaks go off at distracting angles where bikes and cars have gone out of control. These marks don't register until later when I'm standing in the pits I see the skidmarks and bruises and ambulance crew lounging nearby and I realize how serious this activity is.

Riding past a school playground I glance over and see a young girl on a swing. She's swinging confidently, weightless at the top of her arc. I think my connection to the motorcycle is as simple as this.

THIS SITUATION IS SOMETHING I'VE ALWAYS THOUGHT TO BE NORMAL. TO LIVE WITH A THOUGHT DRIFTING IN AND OUT OF FOCUS IN MY MIND. I TRUST THAT UNDER THE RIGHT CIRCUMSTANCES THE THOUGHT WILL CRYSTALLIZE INTO LANGUAGE OR IMAGE. SOMETHING I CAN PUT OUT AND REFLECT ON. I SUPPOSE THAT A THOUGHT THAT'S GONE HAS JUST DRIFTED DEEPER DOWN OR FARTHER OFF TO THE SIDE SOMEWHERE. I CAN SOMETIMES ROOT AROUND AND PULL IT OUT OF THERE LIKE A LOST SOCK.

This situation is something I've always thought to be inevitable. To live with a thought drifting in and out of focus in my mind. I trust that under the right circumstances the thought will crystalize into language or image, something I can put out and reflect on. I suppose that a thought that's gone has just drifted deeper down or farther off to the side somewhere. I can sometimes root around and pull it out of there like a lost sock.

It's curious how noisy this existence is. There's so much going on. So much to anticipate and encounter. You don't look back or you'll be surprised. You must predict and react. Everything is forward, propelling, moving. When the noise and confusion stops the senses seem to open up and the contrast is evident, but you go back out there again. Maybe because it's about going from one to the other and not either one alone.

An image comes to mind as I ride my motorcycle down Route 84 into Connecticut. That image is of a Paul Klee etching of two gnarled old men bent over looking at each other. I think the title is "Two Men Confronting Each Other Supposing the Other to Be of Higher Rank." This image, or more particularly, this title really describes the relationship of most men on motorcycles to other men on motorcycles.

I had just passed a rider on a four lane highway going the other way. He was on a Japanese super bike. A kind of aerodynamic shell with a rider on top. A brightly colored "crotch rocket" that looks fast even standing still. I had looked long enough at him coming the other way to establish eye contact but neither of us acknowledged the other until I waved as he passed. He just looked at me and went by. I cursed to myself in my helmet and thought about this ritual I was participating in.

much as I once did. Want
to know where I want to go
& where I am. It's a solo
trip, spiralling away from
some place, some centere that
I am spiralling outward from
as I grow older—I'm trying
to keep track of this trip. Is
it enough to have made it though?
Is there more that I can do?
Why am I afraid?

An image comes to mind as I ride my motorcycle down Route 34 into Connecticut. That image is of a Paul Klee etching of two grizzled old men bent over glaring at each other. I think the title is "Two Men Confronting Each Other, Supposing the Other to be of Higher Rank." This image, the title particularly, this title really expresses the relationship of most men on motorcycles to other men on motorcycles.

I had just passed a rider on a four lane highway going the other way. He was on a Japanese super bike, a kind of aerodynamic shell with a rider on top. A brightly colored crotch rocket that looks fast even standing still. I had faced long enough at him coming the other way to establish eye contact but neither of us acknowledged the other until I waved as he passed. He just looked at me and went by. I cursed to myself in my helmet and thought about this ritual I was participating in.

I feel as if I'm on a boat (or have been on a boat) and I'm not quite sure how much help I need or want to get where I want to go (where is that?). It's a solo trip travelling away from some place, some center that I'm spiralling outward from as I grow older. I'm trying to keep track of this trip. Is it enough to have made it through? Is there more that I can do? Why am I afraid?

I've also thought about how serious living is. How easily we distance ourselves from nature, only later we realize the roughness of being alive. The messy, coarse, primal-simple rawness of life. I've thought about how it is so untamable, so undefined in its reality. Life forms share a vital and ferocious need to fulfill themselves in surprisingly inelegant ways.

What is this then, some kind of magic? Is it art or science that allows one part of an engine to mesh or glide past another, thousands, millions of times? What are those relationships which make this behavior predictable? They must be very specific, very particular, very small.

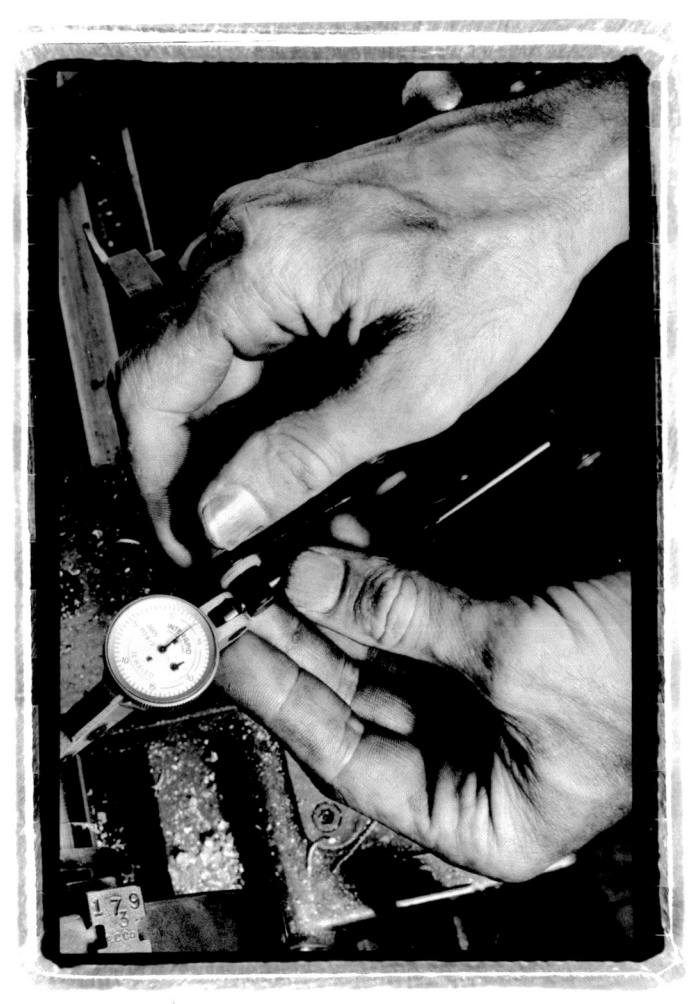

What is this then, some kind of magic? Is it art or science that allows one part of an engine to mesh or glide past another, thousands, millions of times? What are those relationships which make this behavior predictable? They must be very specific, very particular, very small.

Somebody tell me, what is this? I don't want to play anymore. I've been told that life is very simple. Is there an obvious thing sitting right in front of me, blocking my view of the world? So what is this thing that's in my way? What's the payoff for recognizing it, and if it's so easy what do I do with the rest of my life? I worry about that.

Thunder and lightning followed me for the last hour or so of the trip. Over my right shoulder, I could see huge fingers of lightning spreading out and illuminating the valleys as I rode up and down and around the curving roads passing through the slate regions of northeastern Pennsylvania into the farmland farther south.

You don't go for a motorcycle ride to think about something else. When I'm riding I'm focused on my body and the bike. Everything else stops. Everytime my attention waivers I get jolted into realizing that I'm flipping along on a 450 pound gyroscope, I wake up quickly.

I was leaning over it looking closely at the something which is inside the engine, holding onto the handlebars just looking. I relaxed a bit and really started to examine the thing; the frame, the exposed motor, the wires and different scratches and marks. I was recalling in my mind some of the places I had been on the bike. I was playing with the idea of memory imbedded in the bike itself.

I was leaning over it, looking closely at the starter which is inside the engine, holding onto the handlebars just looking. I relaxed a bit and really started to examine the thing; the frame, the exposed motor, the wires and different scratches and marks. I was recalling in my mind some of the places I had been on the bike. I was playing with the idea of memory imbedded in the bike itself.

My first arrival here was mysterious and beautiful. I rode to the northernmost point of settlement, the road ends and I find that I'm riding in the sand. I turned around to go back south, and came upon a car flashing its lights at me. They told me to be careful because of the wild horses that were roaming the road. I must have ridden right through them! While I sat there on the bike about 15 dark horses ambled by, grazing on the bushes. Very quietly they walked across the road and into the darkness.

So here's the story, I'm about 6 years old and I'm riding in the car playing with some toys. The rear window is open and I play in the wind with one of my toy boats. Something happens, a gust of wind, a car passes and the boat flies out of my hand and back behind the car. It's gone in an instant and I will never see it again. The sudden finality of that is so important that I remember this event very clearly.

Since then I've believed that there is a world of lost things where all of the toys go when they fly out of the car window. It's a highway in a barren landscape halfway to the next town. I think of all of my lost things near by the road with the twisted metal & broken glass, unreachable.

I've been told that I lose things so that I can find them again. Maybe so, maybe this is my connection to the world (as someone who has lost something) to find the lost thing means there is continuity, that some things are not final, that I still don't have to choose.

My first moments here were mysterious and exciting. I rode to the northernmost point of settlement. The road ends and I found that I'm riding in the sand. I turned around to go back south and came upon a car shining its lights at me. They told me to be careful because of the wild horses that were roaming the road. I must have ridden right through them. While I sat there on the bike about 15 dark horses ambled by grazing on the bushes. Very quietly they walked across the road and into the darkness.

So here's the story. I'm about 6 years old and I'm riding in the car playing with some toys. The rear window is open and I play in the wind with one of my toy boats. Something happens, a gust of wind, a car passes, and the boat flies out of my hand and back behind the car. It's gone in an instant and I will never see it again. The sudden finality of that is so important that I remember this event very clearly.

Since then I've believed that there is a world of lost things where all of the toys go when they fly out of the car window. It's a highway in a barren landscape halfway to the next town. I think of all of my lost things there by the road with the rusted wire & broken glass, unreachable.

I've been told that I lose things so that I can find them again. Maybe so, maybe this is my connection to the world (as someone who has lost something). To find the lost thing means there is continuity, that some things are not final, that I still don't have to choose.

Sometimes I sing or chant, especially on long stretches. Being able to shift my weight and vocalize allows me to let go of tension. I wonder what I might sound like, going by at 80 miles an hour, yelling as loud as I can.

I remember seeing Harleys go through town, blast over the railroad tracks and stop in front of Chet Glisson's Tavern. I would walk down there and look at the big, shiny beasts with their sheepskin seats and leather saddlebags. How big they were, how much like a horse they were. The width of the tires, the low slung seat and handlebars all reflected power and some secret connection to the road that a boy my age might never know.

Sometimes I sing or chant, especially on long stretches. Being able to shift my weight and vocalize allows me to let go of tension. I wonder what I might sound like, going by at 80 miles an hour, yelling as loud as I can.

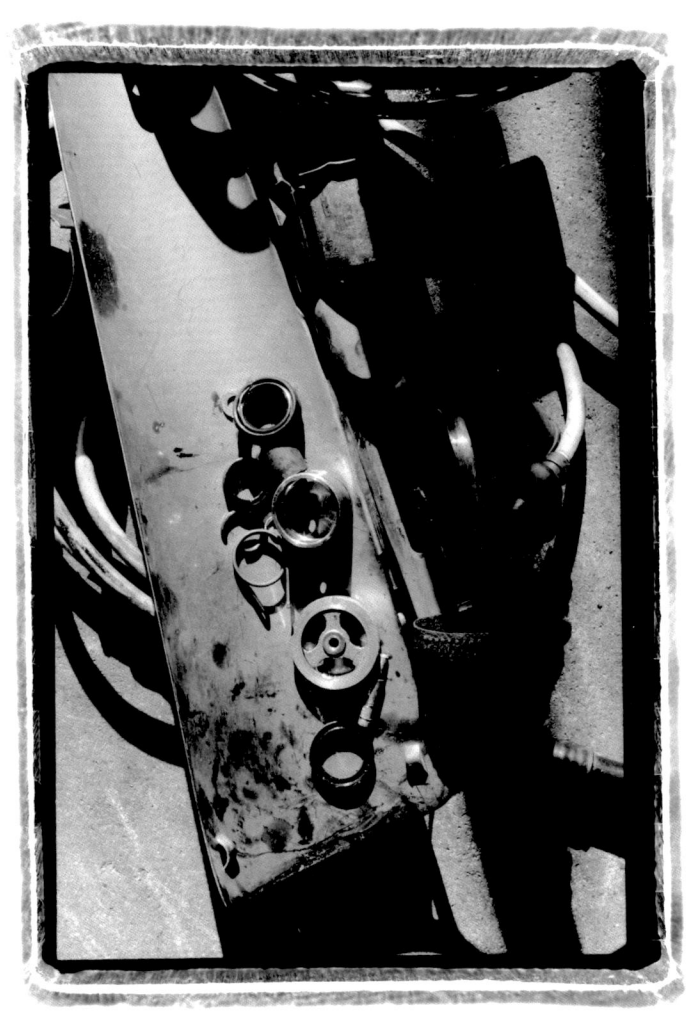

I remember seeing Harleys go through town, blast over the railroad tracks and stop in front of Chet Glisson's tavern. I would walk down there and look at the big, shiny beasts with their sheepskin seats and leather saddlebags. How big they were, how much like a horse they were. The width of the tires, the low slung seat and handlebars all reflected power. And with secret connection to the road that a boy my age might never know.

Shall I talk about fear then? Fear is different every time. Fear crystallizes it boils away all but the most primary impulse. Fear is slow and powerful enough to distort the body over time. Fear isn't about things experienced, it's about things imagined. I think fear is the future.

Shall I talk about fear then?
Fear is different every time. Fear
crystallizes it boils away all but the
most primary impulse. Fear is slow
and powerful enough to distort
the body over time. Fear isn't
about things experienced, its about
things imagined. I think fear
is the future.

MY BIKE IS BACK TOGETHER SO NOW THE 60 OR SO PARTS THAT I HANDLED AND WASHED ARE NOW RECONFIGURED BACK INTO A UNIT. SO I STAND THERE AND STARE AT IT. ALL OF THOSE PARTS ARE HIDDEN YET SOMEHOW TANGIBLY PRESENT NOW THAT I'VE HANDLED THEM.

There's a kind of fatigue that I feel after I've looked at some object or structure that has been dramatically transformed. The feeling gets triggered when I replay in my mind the twisting turning and pulling of the work involved, or when I look at the distortions of tools and the history of marks in the distressed surface.

AND NOW SADNESS, AND HOW I
FEEL THIRSTY WHEN I'M SAD. MY
MOUTH IS DRY AND MY JAW HURTS.
IT'S HARD TO INHALE. MY VOICE IS UNEVEN,
SORT IT FEELS A LOT LIKE FEAR BUT
IT'S MORE IN THE CHEST. I COVER MY
HEAD AND IT HELPS.

There's a kind of fatigue that I feel after I've looked at some object or structure that has been dramatically transformed. The feeling gets triggered when I replay in my mind the twisting, turning and pulling of the work involved, or when I look at the distortions of tools and the history of marks in the distressed surface.

AND NOW SADNESS. AND HOW I
FEEL THIRSTY WHEN I'M SAD MY
MOUTH IS DRY AND MY JAW HURTS.
IT'S HARD TO INHALE. MY VOICE IS UNEVEN,
SOFT. IT FEELS A LOT LIKE FEAR BUT
IT'S MORE IN THE CHEST. I COVER MY
HEAD AND IT HELPS.

It's like walking with someone out on an ever narrowing sandbar into the ocean. Eventually there will be a moment when there is proximity, tension and then contact.

What you learn is that there are multiple ways of knowing, through all of the senses, that motion, sound, sight and smell all contribute to the thing known. And then you want to fix it in your memory.

So you try to sense it again, what usually comes back is a partial image, a fragment of sound a nebulous sense of something, but with too many details to remember. You have the frustrating conviction that it all made sense at the time.

Or is it the other way? That there is too much to know and in the recollection we can sort it all out, change or add or delete so that in a sense we remember selectively.

I think it's the last one that's true. Because the memory is an active sense which tends to make use of other sensory information. The memory provides the structure for how something is known.

I feel a deep knocking that comes from below, up through the ground, a deep shift in things. Not objects but meanings. Something very important has happened to my friend. Now meaning reaches far out. It goes out to the horizon. I stop talking and listen to the deep noise, meaning expands, I think I understand.

I feel a deep knocking
that comes from below,
up through the ground, a
deep shift in things. Not
objects, but meanings.
Something very important
has happened to my friend.
Now meaning reaches far
out. It goes over to the
horizon. I stop thinking and
listen to the deep noise,
meaning expands, I think I
understand.

Title is "Two Men Approaching"

The strange appearance, the other
be of, like one think, the
more particularly, this
seizes the relationship
of the motorcycles to other
superbicycles, they look
hopelessly hopeless, tiger
a land highway of the
up, the snag on a wankski
a vehicle of aerodynamic
a rider on top in helmet
red closed, a rocket that
even standing still, looks
fast enough at him coming of the
to establish one routine
their acknowledged
until happened to we

- *page 5* -

Am I ever prepared for the times when meaning grabs me and shakes me loose? She says these bikes are abandoned, I say they look mysteriously timeless. She says they represent power and speed in repose, I say they look like they emerge from the dark corner of the shed. I am familiar with this place, this state of things collected and put aside, of abundance and sadness at the same time.

- *page 6* -

Riding is like dreaming, projecting yourself forward, focusing outward, sometimes there are so many distractions that the dream is hard to sustain. Moving around the track black streaks go off at distracting angles where bikes and cars have gone out of control. These marks don't register until later when I'm standing in the pits. I see the skidmarks and bruises and the ambulance crew, lounging nearby and I realize how serious this activity is.

- *page 9* -

Riding past a school playground I glance over and see a young girl on a swing. She's swinging confidently, weightless at the top of her arc. I think my connection to the motorcycle is as simple as this.

- *page 14* -

An image comes to mind as I ride my motorcycle down Route 84 into Connecticut. That image is of a Paul Klee etching of two gnarled old men bent over looking at each other. I think the title is "two men confronting each other, each supposing the other to be of higher rank". This image or more particularly, this title really describes the relationship of most men on motorcycles to other men on motorcycles. I had just passed a rider going the other way on a four lane highway. He was on a Japanese superbike, a kind of aerodynamic shell with a rider on top. A brightly colored crotch rocket that looks fast even standing still. I had looked long enough at him to establish eye contact, but neither of us acknowledged the other until I waved as we passed. He just looked at me and went by. I cursed myself in my helmet and thought about this ritual I was participating in.

- *page 10* -

This situation is something I've always thought to be normal. To live with a thought drifting in and out of focus in my mind. I trust that under the right circumstances the thought will crystallize into language or image. Something I can put out and reflect on. I suppose that a thought that's gone has just drifted deeper down or farther off to the side somewhere. I can sometimes root around and pull it out of there like a lost sock.

- *page 13* -

It's curious how noisy this existence is. There's so much going on, so much to anticipate and encounter. You don't look back or you'll be surprised. You must predict and react. Everything is forward propelling, moving. When the noise and confusion stops, the senses seem to open up and the contrast is evident. But you go out back there again, maybe because it's about going from one to the other and not either one alone.

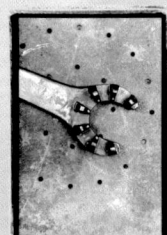

- *page 17* -

I feel as if I'm on a boat (or have been on a boat) and I'm not quite sure how much help I need or want to get where I want to go. (where is that?) It's a solo trip, travelling away from some place, some center that I'm spiralling outward from as I grow older. I'm trying to keep track of this trip. Is it enough to have made it through? Is there more that I can do? Why am I afraid?

- *page 18* -

I've also thought about how serious living is. How easily we distance ourselves from nature. Only later we realize the roughness of being alive. The messy, coarse, primal-simple rawness of life. I've thought about how it is so untamable, so unrefined in it's reality. Life forms share a vital and ferocious need to fulfill themselves in surprisingly inelegant ways.

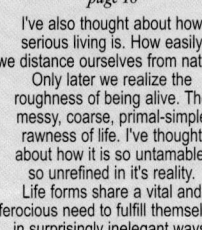

- *page 21* -

What is this then, some kind of magic? Is it art or science that allows one part of an engine to mesh or glide past another, thousands, millions of times? What are these relationships which make this behavior predictable? They must be very specific, very particular, very small.

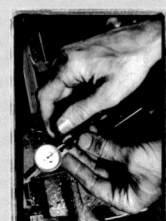

- *page 22* -

Somebody tell me what is this? I don't want to play anymore. I've been told that life is very simple. Is there an obvious thing sitting right in front of me, blocking my view from the world? So what is this thing that's in my way? What's the payoff for recognizing it. And if it's so easy what do I do with the rest of my life? I worry about that.

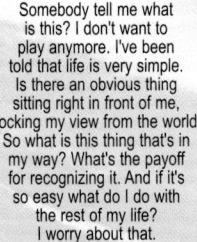

- *page 25* -

Thunder and lightning followed me for the last hour or so of the trip. Over my right shoulder I could see huge fingers of lightning spreading out and illuminating the valleys as I rode up and down and around the curving roads, passing through the slate regions of Northeastern Pennsylvania into the farmland further south.

- *page 26* -

You don't go for a motorcycle ride to think about something else. When I'm riding I'm focused on my body and the bike, everything else stops. Everytime my attention waivers I get jolted into realizing that I'm flipping along on a 450 pound gyroscope. I wake up quickly.

- page 29 -

I was leaning over it. Looking closely at the starter which is inside the engine. I was holding onto the handlebars, just looking. I relaxed a bit and really started to examine the thing; the frame, the exposed motor, the wires, different scratches and marks. I was recalling in my mind some of the places I had been on the bike. I was playing with the idea of memory embedded in the bike itself.

- page 30 -

My first arrival here was mysterious and beautiful. I rode into the northernmost point of settlement, the road ends and I find that I'm riding in the sand. I turned around to go back south and came upon a car flashing it's lights at me. They told me to be careful because of the wild horses that were roaming the road. I must have ridden right through them. While I sat there on the bike about 15 dark horses ambled by, grazing on the bushes. Very quietly they walked across the road and into the darkness.

- page 33 -

So here's the story, I'm about six years old and I'm riding in the car, playing with some toys. The rear window is open and I play in the wind with one of my toy boats. Something happens, a gust of wind, a car passes and the boat flies out of my hand and back behind the car. It's gone in an instant and I will never see it again. The sudden finality of that is so important that I remember this event very clearly. Since then, I've believed that there is a world of lost things where all of the toys go when they fly out of the car window. It's a highway in a barren landscape, halfway to the next town. I think of all of my lost things there by the road with the rusted parts and broken glass, unreachable. I've been told that I lose things so that I can find them again, maybe so, maybe this is my connection to the world (as someone who has lost something). To find the lost thing means there is continuity, that somethings are not final, that I still don't have to choose.

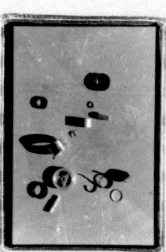

- page 34 -

Sometimes I sing or chant especially on long stretches. Being able to shift my weight and vocalize allows me to let go of tension. I wonder what I might sound like, going by at 80 miles an hour, yelling as loud as I can.

- page 37 -

I remember seeing Harleys go through town, blast over the railroad tracks and stop in front of Chet Glisson's Tavern. I would walk down there and look at the big shiny beasts with their sheepskin seats and leather saddlebags, How big they were, the width of the tires, the low slung seat and handlebars all reflected power and some secret connection to the road that a boy my age might never know.

- page 38 -

Shall I talk about fear then? Fear is different every time. Fear crystallizes, it boils away all but the most primary impulse. Fear is slow and powerful enough to distort the body over time. Fear isn't about things experienced, it's about things imagined. I think fear is the future.

- page 41 -

My bike is back together, so now the sixty or so parts that I handled and washed are now reconfigured back into a unit. So I stand there and stare at it, all of those parts are hidden yet somehow tangibly present now that I've handled them.

- page 42 -

There's a kind of fatigue that I feel after I've looked at some object or structure that has been dramatically transformed. The feeling gets triggered when I replay in my mind the twisting, turning and pulling of the work involved. Or when I look at the distortions of tools and the history of images in the distressed surface.

- page 45 -

And now sadness, and how I feel thirsty when I'm sad, my mouth is dry and my jaw hurts. It's hard to inhale, my voice is uneven, soft. It feels a lot like fear but it's more in the chest. I cover my head and it helps.

- page 49 -

What you learn is that there are multiple ways of knowing. Through all the senses, that motion, sound, sight and smell all contribute to the thing known and then you want to fix it in your memory. So you try to sense it again, what usually comes back is a partial image, a fragment of sound, a nebulous sense of something, but with too many details to remember. You have the frustrating conviction that it all made sense at the time. Or is it the other way? That there is too much to know and in the recollection we can sort it all out, change or add or delete so that in a sense we remember selectively. I think it's the last one that's true. Because the memory is an active sense which tends to make use of other sensory information. The memory provides the structure for how something is known.

- page 46 -

It's like walking with somebody out on an ever narrowing sandbar into the ocean. Eventually there will be a moment when there is proximity, tension and then, contact.

- page 50 -

I feel a deep knocking that comes from below up through the ground, a deep shift in things. Not objects, but meanings. Something very important has happened to my friend. Now meaning reaches far out. It goes out to the horizon. I stop talking and listen to the deep noise, meaning expands, I think I understand.

WITHDRAWN
No longer the property of the
Boston Public Library.
Sale of this material benefits the Library.